Management Alert

The Master Management Series

William F. Christopher
Editor-in-Chief

1

Management Alert

Don't Reform—Transform!

Michael J. Kami

PRODUCTIVITY PRESS

Portland, Oregon

Volume 1 of the *Management Master Series*.
William F. Christopher, Editor-in-Chief
Copyright © 1994 by Productivity Press, Inc.

Productivity Press
P.O. Box 13390
Portland OR 97213-0390
United States of America
Telephone: 503-235-0600
Telefax: 503-235-0909

ISBN: 1-56327-064-1

Book design by William Stanton
Composition by Rohani Design
Printed and bound by BookCrafters in the United States of America

Library of Congress Cataloging-in-Publication Data

Kami, Michael J., 1922–
     Management alert : don't reform--transform! / Michael J. Kami.
        p.   cm. -- (Management master series ; v. 1)
     ISBN 1-56327-064-1
     1. Executive ability. 2. Chief executive officers.
3. Organizational change. 4. Industrial management. 5. Personnel
management. I. Title. II. Series.
HD38.2.K363   1994
658.4'09--dc20   94-27917
                                                                              CIP

98 97 96 95   10 9 8 7 6 5 4 3 2

— CONTENTS —

PUBLISHER'S MESSAGE

The *Management Master Series* was designed to discover and disseminate to you the world's best concepts, principles, and current practices in excellent management. We present this information in a concise and easy-to-use format to provide you with the tools and techniques you need to stay abreast of this rapidly accelerating world of ideas.

World class competitiveness requires managers today to be thoroughly informed about how and what other internationally successful managers are doing. What works? What doesn't? and Why?

Management is often considered a "neglected art." It is not possible to know how to manage before you are made a manager. But once you become a manager you are expected to know how to manage and to do it well, right from the start.

One result of this neglect in management training has been managers who rely on control rather than creativity. Certainly, managers in this century have shown a distinct neglect of workers as creative human beings. The idea that employees are an organization's most valuable asset is still very new. How managers can inspire and direct the creativity and intelligence of everyone involved in the work of an organization has only begun to emerge.

Perhaps if we consider management as a "science" the task of learning how to manage well will be easier. A scientist begins with an hypothesis and then runs experiments to observe whether the hypothesis is correct. Scientists depend on detailed notes about the experiment—the timing, the ingredients, the amounts—and carefully record all results as they test new hypotheses. Certain things come to be known by this method; for instance, that water always consists of one part oxygen and two parts hydrogen.

We as managers must learn from our experience and from the experience of others. The scientific approach provides a model for learning. Science begins with vision and desired outcomes, and achieves its purpose through observation, experiment, and analysis of precisely recorded results. And then what is newly discovered is shared so that each person's research will build on the work of others.

Our organizations, however, rarely provide the time for learning or experimentation. As a manager, you need information from those who have already experimented and learned and recorded their results. You need it in brief, clear, and detailed form so that you can apply it immediately.

It is our purpose to help you confront the difficult task of managing in these turbulent times. As the shape of leadership changes, the *Management Master Series* will continue to bring you the best learning available to support your own increasing artistry in the evolving science of management.

We at Productivity Press are grateful to William F. Christopher and our staff of editors who have searched out those masters with the knowledge, experience, and ability to write concisely and completely on excellence in management practice. We wish also to thank the individual volume authors; Cheryl Rosen and Diane Asay, project managers; Julie Zinkus, manuscript editor; Karen Jones, managing editor; Lisa Hoberg, Mary Junewick, and Julie Hankin, editorial support; Bill Stanton, design and production management; Susan Swanson, production coordination; Rohani Design, composition.

Norman Bodek
Publisher

PREFACE

When I was asked to write a relatively short piece about key changes in management of today's enterprises, there appeared, at first glance, a large array of topics. Upon reflection, the choices narrowed to just two. The first and most important influence on the success or failure of a business is the top power holder. A business organization, by definition, is not a democratic institution. The buck begins and stops at the CEO level. That's where full understanding of the new world situation must begin. There also resides the ultimate responsibility for strategy, action, and results. CEOs and their executive teams must change their ways, adapt faster, act differently, and perform better. But they can't do it alone. Thus, the second most important topic must be about people: the managers and the employees. They also must undergo a revolution, carefully orchestrated and implemented by top management through new organization, better training, and broader empowerment.

The material for this book was gathered from personal experience as a consultant to many diverse corporations and through direct contacts with CEOs. I also strongly believe in continuous gathering of information and clues of change by scanning hundreds of magazines, newspapers, and business and trade publications from all over the world.

My message is a sincere attempt to help the reader adjust better to the fast-changing philosophies, strategies, and operations of a business.

— Michael J. Kami

> *I never give them hell. I just tell the truth and they think it's hell.*
>
> Harry Truman

1

THE NEW CEO

It would be redundant and a firm grasp of the obvious to dwell on the fast-changing world and its effects on business, corporations, and management. The recent difficulty of the past stalwarts of global success—GM, IBM, Sears, Kodak, and Daimler-Benz, to mention just a few—is evidence enough that successful practices of the past don't apply today.

RECOMMENDATIONS TO THE CEO

The following are my recommendations to CEOs. Future success of the enterprise requires the Chief Executive Officer to pursue a philosophy and style of management geared to the brave new world.

1. Forget the past. Prior success breeds complacency and creates roadblocks to constructive change. *Don't look back for answers.*

2. *Think globally.* There's no *American* industry. Money, talent, knowledge, technology, information, products, and services are global, not national, commodities.

3. Internal change must be drastic. One needs *transformation*, not reformation. Often, only a crisis creates the ready climate for revolutionary changes. Usually, by then, it's too late. You

must create powerful internal motivation and a pseudo-crisis environment, to successfully implement the desired drastic revolution/transformation of your business.

4. Base your business on *knowledge* and *information*, not on *things*. Most of your equipment, products, and facilities are obsolete or obsolescent. Up-to-date competence of your people is your only valuable asset.

5. Form *partnerships*. Become allied with marketers, suppliers, distributors, and subcontractors across the globe. Outsource and join strategic alliances.

6. Create an *information-based* organization. It requires direct access to on-line, current, comprehensive databases and electronic communications inside and outside the company.

7. Reduce organizational levels. *Flatten* your organization for faster feedback.

8. Compress *time*. Speed up all your decisions, implementation, actions, and reactions. Make it part of a new culture and new management practices throughout the organization.

9. Concentrate on *core competencies* in your business. That's your most valuable resource. It means you're successfully applying the most current, innovative, state-of-the-art knowledge in some parts of your business. Capitalize on this *core*, keep it current, keep it unique. Subcontract the rest.

10. Prepare personnel for change in *global* markets and activities. Continuously train all employees to improve their knowledge and skills. They must learn new ways, new systems, new techniques, and new interpersonal

skills. They must better understand other languages, other cultures, different political systems, and different business environments.

11. *Empower* your employees. Delegate authority, responsibility, and accountability down to the grass roots. Rely on teamwork and cooperation.

12. *Manage talent.* Find, hire, keep, and promote talented people. Encourage innovation at all levels of the organization. Don't be afraid of gorillas: They are talented, creative people, difficult to manage and different from others. Love them and feed them!

13. Practice global *benchmarking.* Compare your operations to the best in the world. Learn from them and practice continuous improvement.

14. Consider *reengineering.* Reexamine every phase of your operations. If necessary, redesign them from scratch.

15. Redefine your *quality* standards. Start continuous quality improvement programs in all your operations: production, sales, administration, and engineering. Don't tolerate errors. Do it right the first time.

16. Act *outside-in.* Look at your operations through the eyes of customers, suppliers, shareholders, consumers, and society. Don't think or act *inside-out.*

Traits of the New CEO

Modern executives must actively prepare to successfully implement all the above recommendations. My ideal CEO would become:

- *Global strategist*: The executive must feel at home in the international environment. This includes in-depth understanding of business practices in many countries. It requires knowledge of international trade, exports, imports, licensing, bartering, joint ventures, tariffs, and multinational deals. The executive must think and act globally, not nationally. It's a hard psychological adjustment after years of unchallenged economic dominance by U.S. firms and U.S. management techniques.

- *Knowledgeable technologist*: The executive must really understand modern technology, new techniques, and new specifications. Ten-minute briefings on major breakthroughs will not suffice. Allocation of resources to new technology, in times of explosive change, is a difficult and risky task that requires top-executive attention and in-depth understanding.

- *Astute diplomat*: Governments will become more involved in business, not less. Executives must deal with nonmarket forces such as regulations, treaties, legal requirements, litigation, tariffs, and other barriers throughout the world. Personal multinational negotiations require diplomatic skill, empathy with diverse cultures, and familiarity with world finance, politics, and social change.

- *Leader*: A different type of leadership will be required. The commander-in-chief is being replaced by the coach. Consensus building and genuine teamwork will take precedence over direct orders and unilateral decisions. Communication skills are essential as organizations decentralize. Larger span of control because of fewer management levels requires better, faster, and more direct dialogue with the grass roots. These are not easy tasks. The leader must be genuine. Manipulation, power politics, underhanded tactics, and empty promises will not work!

Are these superhuman characteristics? Not really. Super-CEOs are still rare, but they do exist. There are many excellent companies today. Unfortunately, they're not the same as the excellent companies listed by Tom Peters and Robert H. Waterman in their super-seller *In Search of Excellence*, in the early '80s. Too many executives stopped listening and learning. They withered and so did their companies.

> *The worst mistakes in business are made in good times, not bad times.*
>
> Tom Watson, Jr., IBM

SPEED, CHANGE, AND STRESS

Today's key to success is to make faster, better decisions that lead to faster, better actions. The speedup factor should be 4x. This means executives must make decisions and complete actions four times faster than in the past. What took four years, we must do in one year. What took a year, we must complete in three months. What took a quarter, we should finish in less than a month. What took a month, we now execute in a week. Whatever task needed a week shouldn't need more than a day! It also means that executive conflict and anxiety may increase proportionally to the speedup. The resulting stress could cause the new decision and execution system to produce worse results than the slower *business-as-usual* methods.

Achieving the 4x decision speedup requires reorganizing business operations to cope with uncertainty. This entails much more than just catchy slogans. Walking around may have to accelerate to *running* around. Managers must be coached and motivated. Joint strategies must be orchestrated and negotiated. Executives must be continually on the move. The stress increases exponentially. Many more intricate interrelationships lead to inevitable line and staff conflicts. Disputes about responsibility and accountability will be common and unpleasant.

Executives must be psychologically prepared for new realities of rising management pressures. Their stress levels will reach intolerable conditions unless they're able to adjust. Today's leaders:

1. Must inspire and motivate people from around the world to work together and achieve higher objectives.

2. Must develop multicultural understanding and adapt naturally to various world cultures, feeling at home in any environment.

3. Must see the things invisible, anticipate change and love it.

4. Must acquire knowledge through a lifelong, continuous program of learning and self-renewal.

5. Must become computer literate to understand and intelligently access databases.

6. Must be at ease in personal communications and capable of effective and fast resolution of conflicts.

7. Must have the coaching and teaching ability to transfer and exchange personal knowledge and experience.

8. Must be prepared for constant travel, living out of a suitcase, ignoring jet lag, being always on the move and liking it.

9. Must adapt rapidly to unexpected changes in schedules, priorities, and results.

10. Must develop flexible minds that easily switch between the analytical and the intuitive, the long and short-range, and the rational and irrational.

A personal, thoughtful self-analysis is essential. CEOs, owners, top executives must ask themselves a crucial question: *Am I ready for this and do I really want it?* If the real answer is no, the executives will experience a growing and excessive stress. It will make them less effective. It will impair their ability to cope with business pressures. Professional life will be inseparable from personal life. Keeping the proper balance will be very difficult.

> *Choose a job you love, and you will never have to work a day in your life.*
>
> Confucius

THE ROLE OF INTUITION IN TOP MANAGEMENT DECISIONS

The dictionary definition of intuition is *the process of attaining knowledge without reasoning*. Business shouldn't be run by the roll of the dice, but the *smell* test method has its place. The expression was coined thirty years ago by Al Williams, then president of IBM. It's a search for small clues or seemingly insignificant events that alert one's mind to a possibility, an opportunity, a warning, or a potential new trend. The process requires detection, analysis, *lateral* thinking, and extrapolation without applying rigorous proof. Trend leaders are people who are good at *seeing things invisible*, ahead of common wisdom. Executives should not be afraid of using their intuition. It must be partly based, however, on deductive reasoning from observation of reality. The increased necessity for *speed management* will make intuitive conclusions necessary to avoid *paralysis by analysis* and missing the boat. Making fast decisions will increase business risks, but making decisions too late will be even costlier and sometimes fatal.

Using intuition requires practice. Here are two examples of the smell test as warning:

- In 1984, Sears headquarters ordered a local store to move its mail-order pickup from a convenient drive-in, ground-floor location to a second-story area, farthest away from the escalator. The rationale was to force customers to walk through the store, expecting additional impulse buying.

    ➤ Smell test: Sears acted as an inside-out company: selfish, self-centered, unresponsive to customer needs and wants.

    ➤ Conclusion: The customer is not important to Sears and the attitude permeates the entire organization. Statistically, it's an invalid extrapolation. But it's a valid smell test. Giant Sears did get in deep trouble when it was unable to meet customer-oriented competition.

- In 1987, Mercedes-Benz substituted aluminum for stainless steel in a small windshield-washer-spray part on its 560SL convertible. The savings were a few cents on a very expensive car. Aluminum corroded in salty air and blocked water flow, making the window washer inoperative.

➤ Smell test: Mercedes sacrificed its biggest asset, very high quality perception by customers, for petty cost savings.

➤ Conclusion: A statistically invalid extrapolation indicated that the company image would be impaired, new Japanese competition would carve out big chunks of the market, and profits would plummet. Mercedes-Benz sales first declined, then plummeted.

Some such observations may appear trivial. I, personally, form a strong negative impression when an executive doesn't have a fax number printed on his/her stationery. Is the management in such a company really progressive and responsive to changing conditions? A business can apply the smell test to observe seemingly unimportant trivia about quality of goods and services, productivity, housekeeping, bureaucracy, telephone manners, customer complaints, managerial attitudes, replies to letters, employee quips, and behavior. The smell test can be developed by practice and refined by critical appraisal. It's certainly not a scientific method of analysis, but it provides a high batting average for early detection of important trends. A company should practice, encourage and refine the smell test on a continuous basis.

Common sense is genius dressed in its working clothes.

Ralph Waldo Emerson

GLOBAL EXECUTIVE IGNORANCE

The biggest shortcoming of world executives is, unequivocally, the lack of self-imposed discipline for continuous self-education. World knowledge doubles every four years; soon it will be every three years. Thus, every manager automatically becomes obsolete within a very short time, unless he/she makes a serious and determined effort, consistently and constructively, to remain current and knowledgeable.

Staying Current

Every thinking person and, particularly, people with high responsibilities should commit to a personal priority of continuous self-renewal. Fast-changing conditions and events require thoughtful preparation and daily training to learn about, adapt to, and cope with new impacts. Staying current must become a self-improvement program, a daily mental exercise practiced every single day, for the rest of one's life. Discipline is as important as the practice of proper daily diet and physical exercise. Obviously discipline is difficult to achieve, as evidenced by the many flabby managers, who have little willpower. Such essential, vital regimens are often neglected or postponed *ad infinitum*. While it's really tough at the beginning, it becomes fun with practice. Opening one's mind to new horizons and maintaining one's competence should be job number one for every manager, including the CEO! A serious program for keeping up with current changes would be as follows:

- Read and clip five newspapers each day, for example, the local paper, *The New York Times*, *The London Times*, *The Financial Times*, and *The Wall Street Journal*.

- Subscribe to, scan, read, and clip each issue of at least twenty business-oriented magazines from around the world, such as *The Economist* and *Business Week.*

- Read, in depth, one non-fiction book a month. Select it from the *Executive Book Summaries* which provides monthly abstracts of the latest books on business, management, economics, and society.

- Yearly, attend an intensive three-week refresher course in your discipline at a serious and reputable center of learning.

- Learn another language well enough to speak and read it fluently.

- Become computer literate at the office and at home. Use a computer to save time, enlarge your knowledge, and communicate with others. Be able to access internal and external databases for instant access to vast sources of vital information.

- Expand your present expertise to additional fields to acquire multi-disciplinary knowledge.

- Spend more time out of your office. Visit operations at odd hours (early morning, late night). Practice MBWA (management by walking around) and MBWO (management by walking outside).

Staying Open

The higher the executives' positions, the less education they seem to seek. Yet they're the ones who need it most. They should become examples to others within their organization. The most common excuse is lack of time. That's ridiculous! Maintaining one's competence and the infusion of new knowledge are essential for better management in an era of fast change and unpredictability.

Many executives and managers are arrogant. They actually believe they know it all. They have *arrived* and don't need to study because their jobs are to manage and lead subordinates. They rationalize that their roles are *not* to know the details. Other managers are willing to learn, but are so pressured by daily crises that they keep postponing their reeducation. Both kinds become dinosaurs and contribute to the decay and the eventual demise of the business. Benjamin Disraeli wrote: *To be conscious that you are ignorant of the facts is a great step to knowledge.*

It would be a great step forward if executives would adopt a new mindset: to love knowledge and hate the status quo, to love technology and hate bureaucracy, to love the future and hate the past, to love speed and hate waiting, to love global and hate provincial, to love pluralism and hate uniformity!

If a little knowledge is dangerous, where is the person who has so much as to be out of danger?

T.H. Huxley

FOCUS AND FLEXIBILITY

Focus is a corporate buzzword that means many things: stick to your knitting, get rid of lemon acquisitions, cut unprofitable lines, go back to basics, concentrate on the winners. Sounds simplistic, yet it's good advice. Companies wouldn't have to *restructure* if they had stayed focused in the first place. Diversification was popular for a long time. Big companies kept increasing the average number of businesses they were in by factors of three and four times. Today, there's a fundamental reversal. The number of single-business companies doubled in the last decade. The general trend is away from diversification, back to core operations.

Consultants recommend basic changes in companies' *culture*, a lengthy and difficult process. Peter Drucker has better advice: *Don't change culture, change habits!* Be pragmatic. Set new, usually faster, standards for all your operations: processing orders, producing goods, testing the market, handling complaints. Work on the tangible, not on the esoteric.

Along with focus, add *flexibility*, to create a recipe for good management in the '90s. Flexibility means being nimble and allowing local people to respond rapidly to local conditions without bureaucratic hindrance from the top. It means empowering your employees, after you train them and remove their dependency on orders from remote bosses. It means using more subcontractors to help offset increased risks of internal overcapacity. It suggests strategic alliances to help each other with *core competencies*. It implies getting closer to customers to understand and satisfy their changing needs. It requires a fluid organization where people work together on different teams and task forces to solve problems and make improvements, in addition to their normal job routines.

Difficult? Yes. Vital? Yes. Achievable? Absolutely. It requires a determined mindset, a focused direction, and *Monday-morning*, *action-oriented* people. The best-managed companies have done it. Wal-Mart Stores, Rubbermaid, Merck, Procter & Gamble, and 3M are the perennial examples on how to run a business. You can do it whether you are small, big, or medium-sized. You not only can do it, you *must* do it.

> *Don't be afraid to take a big step when one is indicated. You can't cross a chasm in two small jumps.*
>
> David Lloyd George

REAL WORLD AWARENESS

The complexity of running any organization, large or small, has increased tremendously in the past ten years. There are many tough problems with production, productivity, marketing, technology, and personnel. These are not the fault of the managers in charge. They're the result of inertia and growing incompetence in the top managers who run the company. Helmuth von Moltke, a Prussian general of the nineteenth century, was ahead of his time when he formulated the strategy for today's complexity and unpredictability: *Strategy is not a lengthy action plan. It is rather the evolution of a central idea through continually changing circumstances.* A CEO and all the top managers must deeply feel, understand, and be at ease with the new concepts of the '90s. The implementation of change must be part of their normal operating ways— a pleasure, not an ordeal.

Part of the process is to be closer to the operations— to the real world. *Management by walking around*, which Peters and Waterman introduced in *In Search of Excellence*, was recently upgraded by Peter Drucker. He suggests that the most important role of executives is not walking around their own operations, but outside their domain. It makes remarkable sense that a company with a 10 percent market share should pay much more attention to why 90 percent of potential customers are not buying from them. The executives should talk more to the noncustomers, nondealers, and nonusers to find out why they do business somewhere else. It's not enough to accumulate market research data, focus-group conclusions, and sales department analyses or excuses. A thinking executive will schedule regular visits and chats with people buying or selling competitors' products and services. It should become a practice and a habit. *Management by walking outside* means to *case the joint* personally and learn by first-hand experience. Don't always rely on data and statistics. Many situations must be experienced and felt.

> *Everything should be made as simple as possible, but not simpler.*
>
> Albert Einstein

DECENTRALIZATION AND HORIZONTAL ORGANIZATION

One could ask whether the present rush towards decentralization is a valid and permanent trend or a consultant's fad. Will the pendulum effect swing companies back to centralization, and how soon? In my opinion, decentralization is a must for survival in today's and in future environments. The explosion of knowledge increased the number of choices available to managers by several orders of magnitude. The resulting complexity delays effective decision making, in times when *compression of time* and faster reaction are essential for competitive success. The only solution is to reduce the complexity of the whole by breaking it into smaller, more manageable, quasi-autonomous parts, linked by modern communications technology. Small networked computers are the key. They replace the large mainframes that forced centralization in the past.

The Horizontal Organization

Smaller units will use *knowledge workers* with minimal hierarchy and reporting levels. The same or more work will be done by 20 to 50 percent fewer people. Success will depend on the ability and willingness of the units to communicate freely with their counterparts. This is where superior leadership becomes essential. Each unit must be much more focused, less vertically integrated, and have greater freedom of action. Such a horizontal organization, based on information and communications rather than control, will require talented people to be differently motivated. Upward mobility will be limited because management has fewer layers. Work satisfaction, *fraction-of-the-action*, and broader equity participation must replace previous methods of reward based on promotions and title enhancements.

A lot has been said and written about the merits of the horizontal organization. Common buzzwords are: customer-oriented, total-quality focused, empowered work force, continuous improvement, self-directed, teamwork-based, flat, fast, and flexible. Frank Ostroff and Douglas Smith have done an excellent analysis on the subject in *The McKinsey Quarterly* 1992, number 1.

The traditional vertical organization is based on combining similar tasks under one leadership to achieve functional excellence in the particular operation. Managerial emphasis is on individual performance. The major problem with a vertical organization is the difficulty of coordinating different functions. Optimization of each part does not guarantee the optimization of the whole.

How the Horizontal Organization Functions

The horizontal organization is set up by business processes and work flows directed to the needs of an ultimate user: customer, supplier, or distributor. Managerial emphasis is on team performance.

- Organize around a process, not around a task. Identify the four or five *core (key) processes* in your business. Organize to perform everything that's necessary, in sequence, to satisfy the ultimate user—the customer. Best performance is achieved by teams working together, *passing the baton*, to finally gain the desired measure of customer satisfaction.

- Flatten the hierarchy by combining related tasks. *Emphasize flow* and try to reduce to a minimum the number of activities that divide the core process. Maintain a continuous flow of sequential tasks.

- Assign *ownership* of processes and process performance to a team. The team (not exceeding 15 to 20 people) manages, directs, and supervises up to thousands of people involved in the *delivery*.

- Link performance and evaluation to the *satisfaction of the customer*. There's a big difference between superior internal performance and whether the customer likes it.

- Teams must have the *ability, responsibility*, and *authority* to make decisions. Avoid separation of decision making from implementation. Provide the team members with access to any company information and databases they deem necessary to achieve their best performance.

- Concentrate on *team building*: multitasking, multicompetence, cross-training, use of complementary skills. Train for multiple competencies as a rule, not an exception. Broad competence is the first and primary requirement. Training, education, and updating must become a continuous process, an integral part of any job.

- Maximize contact with the *outside world*: customers, public, suppliers. Involve them fully in your operations by asking for advice, suggestions, and criticisms. Team members should engage in a continuous dialogue with the end users.

- Reward *team performance*, not individual performance. A superior team performance depends on individuals being able to work together towards one main goal: satisfying the needs of the end user.

Horizontal organization is not a set of boxes that contain names and titles, neatly linked by solid or dotted lines on a one-dimensional piece of paper. It's a live process, a dynamic flow of operations geared to a well-defined aim and a measurable outcome. It's a philosophy of human interaction, teamwork, and cooperation. It's an action-oriented, result-geared, *living organization*.

Progress is impossible without change; and those who cannot change their minds, cannot change anything.

George Bernard Shaw

LONG-RANGE PLANS

Remember when it was fashionable to emulate the *sophisticated* companies who employed long-range planners and each spring prepared five-year and even ten-year plans? Remember when *vision, mission,* and *long-term goals and objectives* were revered buzzwords? Today, skeptics define long-range plans as asking "what's for lunch?" Many executives dismiss long-range planning as a futile exercise because of extremely fast-changing conditions, global unpredictability, and short life cycles for products and services. Common wisdom says that technological breakthroughs and worldwide competition create a compression of obsolescence, invalidating any planning process beyond a one- or two-year horizon.

That's wrong! It's *because* we live in an era of unpredictable change and time compression that we *must* plan long range.

The New Process of Long-Range Planning

The process and the contents of today's plans must be much different than in the past. Classic long-range planning was based on immovable five-year objectives, detailed forecasts of sales of present and future products/services, and economic assumptions, presuming little change from the current status quo. Financial projections of P&L were based on continuous improvement of all factors and ratios of the business, culminating in spectacular revenues, margins, and profits at the end of the fifth year. That euphoria is over. Here is a realistic and practical new process for long-range plans.

1. Set a few basic assumptions. Consider the following:

➤ Unpredictability will continue.

➤ Technological breakthroughs will occur at a fast pace.

➤ Businesses in industrial and developing countries will continue to be highly competitive.

➤ Societies will become even more pluralistic.

If you believe the above conditions will prevail, the long-range planning process must be directed to prepare a business enterprise to deal with these realities.

2. Establish desirable internal goals and objectives that are not cast in concrete. They represent a base direction that we know will be modified because of changing conditions, but they serve as a reference point for orderly changes of operations and policies.

3. Teams from all parts of the business must propose many innovative *action programs* for major phases of the business (development, production, marketing, service). Purpose: to change present operations *(business as usual)* to the desired future levels of revenue and profitability. As most programs have different time frames for completion, a long-range plan should roll forward without a fixed length of time.

4. Because we know that unexpected events will occur, we must calculate the costs and devise means of *reversibility* for all programs and operations. If the cost of reversal (cancellation) is prohibitively large, we should not start that particular program, even if it appears a sure thing.

5. Don't even look at a program proposal unless it contains three distinct *alternatives* of actions and policies to achieve similar results. This gives management a menu of choices. It also shows the degree of imagination and flexibility of the people involved in the planning process.

6. The long-range plan must specifically identify *flexibility* as a *major management objective.* Preparing for flexibility must become a continuous, long-range, high-priority process. To meet this crucial need requires program proposals to contribute to:

➤ faster decision making

➤ faster implementation

➤ better, faster data

➤ better, faster communications

➤ flatter organization

➤ decisions at lower levels (delegation)

➤ faster throughput (from order to delivery)

➤ reduction of red tape and bureaucracy.

Don't set absolute objectives. Plan by programs, not by forecasts. Calculate costs of reversibility of decisions. Demand proposals to achieve greater flexibility. Aim to become fast, fluid, and flexible. You'll gain a major competitive advantage.

Communicating Goals and Strategies

Policy-making executives complain that their objectives and strategies get lost or are misinterpreted down the ladder. Whose fault is it? *There are no bad customers, only bad salespersons.* Top management is guilty of bad communications. Many CEOs utter the right words: participation, delegation, teamwork, flatter organization. But, managers down the line think: one-man rule, autocratic, top-down management, no feedback. To them it's a *different circus, same clowns!* George Bernard Shaw was prophetic about business organizations of the '90s when he wrote: *The greatest problem in communication is the illusion that it has been accomplished.* Here is some advice about communicating within the corporation.

- Objectives and policies proclaimed by top management must be realistic and credible. Otherwise, they are counterproductive. Don't wave the 25 percent ROI flag this year when the operating units' ROI declined from 16 percent to 13 percent last year. Don't proclaim decentralized autonomy, yet control hiring of divisional clerks from corporate headquarters.

- True understanding and conviction about corporate goals and new strategies are not achieved by distribution of four-pound volumes in fancy covers or by an hour-long rah-rah speech by the CEO to all the managers. It takes honest face-to-face and one-on-one personal communication, explanation, exchange of views, coaching, and listening. Do this from level to level, throughout the world, if necessary, with uninhibited upward feedback.

- The stamp of credibility, and the acceptance of goals and performance according to new strategies, will only happen when the line managers actually believe that management is hearing and acting on their feedback. Workers and supervisors anxiously, often desperately, wait and wish for a positive sign. When the *grass roots* realize that someone upstairs really listens to them, sales rapidly increase, and productivity, quality, performance, and morale greatly improve.

You cannot plan the future by the past.

Publius Syrus (40 B.C.)

KEY MEASUREMENTS

Effective executives have key information about the status of their businesses at their fingertips. Every morning they press a button on their terminals to display the ten most important measurements, correct and current, for each of the business units (profit centers) in their companies. A further inquiry displays, for each measurement, historical trends in graph form, highs and lows, and any additional details and comparisons that may be needed. Simple? Yes. Common? No. Very few executives have easy access to a key measurements system. The usual excuse is that no one actually organized a list of the most important indicators. No one asked the executives what they really want. No one told the MIS manager what to provide. I am not talking about the pounds of detailed analyses and financial or operations statements produced daily in any business. I am talking about just ten ratios or calculations to focus attention on the heartbeat of the business.

One key measurement for Harley-Davidson Motorcycle Division is the monthly ratio of new state registrations of Harley bikes to the total registrations of motorcycles above 1000 cc versus similar data on the competitive Honda bikes. Such an index gives an immediate *feel* of the overall market and Harley's position versus its key competitor. Further inquiry could provide historical trend, cumulative data for three months, and breakdown by geographical region, if further details are required.

In another company, one of the key measurements is the ratio of units in dealers' inventories versus daily sales versus factory production, in order to monitor dealers' sales and the production line. A clever human resource measurement is the ratio of voluntary versus involuntary terminations. It may trigger investigation of morale problems or inadequate hiring and training practices in important areas such as engineering or sales. A comparison of final assembly rejects versus warranty claims may yield advance indication of improvement or deterioration of quality control.

The CEO and his top associates should each *individually* prepare a list that shows their selection of their ten most important indicators for each business unit. The group should then meet and *jointly* select a shorter list of clever, important, meaningful measurements, ratios, and comparisons, in order of priority. They must then keep the list current, update it when new data become available, and make it easily accessible for executive use. Support data, graphs, trends, analyses, and conclusions should also be prepared for retrieval in the shortest and most meaningful way. I recommend a shared computer database networked to individual PCs in the executives' offices, cars, and homes.

The important philosophy behind the key measurements is that they provide clues for early detection of major positive or negative trends in the business. The process of designing and selecting the indicators should be done by top executives who run the business, not by clerical or support staff. Business people waste the equivalent of one day a week looking for information they want. Insist on getting it your way!

It's important to remember Pareto's law, the 80/20 rule: 80 percent of the results are usually generated by 20 percent of the cause. In most cases, a few customers generate the most sales, a few parts cause the most inventory problems, a few locations give the biggest headaches, and a small number of employees drive Human Resources crazy. Ask to see reports and measurements based on the 80/20 rule. Avoid looking at trivia.

> *Everybody gets so much information all day that they lose their common sense.*
>
> Gertrude Stein (1946)

BENCHMARKING AND REENGINEERING REVISITED

Find the aspects of your core business that need improvement and prioritize them. Find and study firms that do the items on your list better than anyone else in the world. Contact them, visit them, learn from them, and imitate them. A common mistake is to look for benchmark examples among one's competitors. But access to their information and visits are difficult. Look outside your field. British computer maker ICL used Marks & Spencer (retail chain) as best point of comparison to improve its distribution system. Another firm studied methods used in motor-racing pit-stop procedures, where every second counts, to improve their tool changeovers on the production line. It takes imagination to make the proper connections.

Spurred by magazine articles, books, and hungry consultants, businesses often take a ride on a roller-coaster of enthusiasm and disappointment about new management techniques. We struggled with QC (quality circles), JIT (just-in-time inventory), TQM (total quality management), FMS (flexible manufacturing systems), CI (continuous improvement), CIP (computer-integrated production), and CAD-CAM (computer-aided design and computer-aided manufacturing). The key words now are benchmarking and reengineering. All of the above are important techniques that can bring excellent, even spectacular, results when applied well in places where they fit and are needed. Excesses, hoopla, and poor implementation bring the disappointments.

Benchmarking

Benchmarking is not new. *Learn from the leader* is a classic and valuable practice. When Walter Chrysler tore apart an Oldsmobile to study how it was made, he was practicing benchmarking. A good definition of benchmarking is: the continuous practice of thoroughly measuring a company's products, services, processes, and practices against the best equivalents among global, leading, successful enterprises. The emphasis is on *continuous*, *thorough* and *global*. The best people to involve in studies are those who can make changes in their own operations. Toyota pioneered JIT by studying shelf replenishment in U.S. supermarkets. Southwest Airlines reduced the turnaround time of its aircraft by studying pit crews at the Indy 500. Over 80 percent of Fortune 500 companies practice some form of benchmarking. Independent databases of modern practices are growing and prospering. Action-oriented, properly managed, dedicated benchmarking is a valuable tool and should become common practice in any organization.

Reengineering

Reengineering used to be referred to as *changing the process* and never aspired to become a hype or a quasi-religion. The eternal problem with improving any process (product manufacturing, merchandise deliveries, accounts payable paperwork) is the justifiable fear of disturbing or critically wounding an ongoing operation essential to an ongoing business. That's the reason for *incremental* improvements, or patching here and there. The proponents of process change, or reengineering, say *you must start with a clean sheet of paper*. It makes sense. If you were not in operation and were planning to get into a business, how would you best design all the processes, using modern technology, bold thinking, and very challenging objectives? Start serious homework next Monday morning. The concept is valid, important, and rewarding. Try it first. Select a bottleneck procedure or system in your operations and let the people directly involved in the problem reengineer the flow from *scratch*. You will be pleasantly surprised that often you can achieve big improvements without additional capital investment.

Benchmarking and reengineering go well together. Find how others do a job better, cheaper, and faster. If the comparative gains are large, it's worthwhile to imitate a process or adapt it to your circumstance. To gain the big benefits, your present process will probably need drastic changes. You might as well reengineer, that is, start from scratch. Today's businesses must be globally competitive. They must act and react faster and better to new technology, new competition, and new markets. It doesn't matter whether management techniques are old or new. If they're good, use them fully and boldly. Don't be tentative. Don't be incremental. Don't think 5 percent or 10 percent improvement. Think 50 percent and 100 percent!

Knowledge is the beginning of practice; doing is the completion of knowing.

Wang Yang-Ming (1498)

COST MANAGEMENT

New concepts of management require *executive amnesia*. Forget how you managed yesterday; do it differently and much better today. Companies developing a new product typically design it first, then calculate its cost. If it doesn't meet the cost/price/market criteria, the company redesigns it or targets it for a different, usually smaller, market. A much better way is to target the optimum market price first and work back to the desired costs. All departments involved are requested simultaneously to innovate and meet the cost targets. The planning and design stages are crucial for proper costing. But it requires a team effort of design, engineering, production, manufacturing, service, purchasing, and marketing. Suppliers of parts, materials, and components should also be given target costs early. The Japanese call the process *tataku*, beating down costs.

Reverse cost management, that is, calculating the target before design, also applies to many other activities in the business. Management should establish challenging new cost targets for customer service, promotion and advertising, health care insurance, and employee training. Don't think *cost cutting*, but *cost innovation*. Change the system, the traditional way of doing a task, in order to achieve the same results at a predetermined, targeted lower cost. That's a fundamental difference of approach and execution. *Cost to market, don't market to cost.* And think carefully about how you figure costs. For the way work is done today, traditional cost accounting does not provide numbers you can rely on. Activity Based Costing (ABC) and other new management accounting methods can give you much more reliable decision-support information on costs. In today's world, costing systems also need to change.

> *Get your facts first, and then you can distort them as much as you please.*
>
> Mark Twain

2

PEOPLE

While a major management revolution is sweeping through the executive suites, a major demographic revolution is changing the American work force and workplace. During the '80s a big shift occurred in the utilization of the U.S. work force. Goods-producing employment declined and service employment soared to over 76 percent of all U.S. jobs. Service jobs increased by 19.6 million! The future will have much different labor characteristics. The '80s saw a huge shift of workers between two economic sectors. The '90s produced a revolutionary change of cultural and racial components of our entry-level work force and a revolutionary knowledge demand for all others.

The traditional share of the white male in the U.S. work force will drop to a minority of 39 percent of all workers. The difference is being filled by Hispanic, Black, and Asian men, and women. Adam Smith wrote that *a nation's wealth is its people.* Wealth is produced by applied intelligence and knowledge. Some minorities and immigrants today suffer from inadequate education and training. As our society increases in complexity, so do jobs. An auto mechanic once needed to access and understand 5,000 pages of service manuals. Today the information fills almost 500,000 pages. Use of computerized databases and automated diagnostic machines becomes essential. Below-average skills were sufficient to fill about 40 percent of jobs in the '80s. It's sufficient for only 27 percent during this decade.

ADDRESSING THE WORKPLACE REVOLUTION

The double-edged gap of inadequate public education and massive functional illiteracy, combined with a labor shift toward the poor and underprivileged, must be met by business and private institutions. Counting on the government is pure delusion. Companies must place high priorities on internal training, understanding cultural pluralism, and providing individual, not mass, motivation. The following actions are needed:

- *Understand cultural diversity.* Most corporate cultures and personnel department policies are based on the characteristics of the white male. It's imperative to train managers for multicultural behavior. Different nationalities, races, and sexes respond differently to company instructions, policies, incentives and reprimands. Managers shouldn't transmit executive-suite messages literally down to the grass roots. They must show the ability to interpret, translate, modify, and customize according to the perception and culture of each group of employees. This may sound difficult and even subversive, but the status quo alternative is much worse. All future managers should have multicultural sensitivity. This is even more imperative for businesses with global operations or global aspirations. Today, fewer than 30 percent of U.S. businesses plan special programs for women, immigrants, and minorities who will make up 85 percent of new workers.

- *Train for entry-level.* All other industrial countries and many developing countries provide better schooling and job training for noncollege-bound youth than the U.S. educational system. Although some corporations spend huge sums for training employees, the great majority of businesses—over 80 percent—are not very concerned about basic skills. Shortsighted policy of low wages and high turnover seems to dominate. The obvious answer is to train beginners better and keep them growing rather than churning.

- *Train for multiskilled tasks.* It's an accepted fact that reorganizing work produces large productivity gains. Tiers of managers and supervisors are eliminated and teams of workers make many important focused decisions. Global competition has eroded U.S. market share by perfecting and implementing such multiskill programs. This process, creating high-performance workers, requires training employees in good reading, math, science, and problem-solving skills. Fewer than 10 percent of U.S. companies plan to implement such programs, even as they face global competition.

- *Hire and manage older workers.* Employers should increasingly hire experienced retired workers in traditionally entry-level jobs. It's a great resource of talent. Many myths can be easily dispelled. Older workers display not higher, but much lower, absenteeism. They show up for work in difficult circumstances (e.g., snowstorms) when many of the younger generation stay home. Their potentially slower reflexes and response are countered by prudence, experience, and attention. Their job injury rate is about half that of their juniors.

Contrary to the folklore, they can be creative and are eager to learn. Some of the best computerized CAD-CAM designers are the old-fashioned toolmakers, who combine real job experience with new technologies. It's a question of individualized attention and motivation, directed at the specific characteristics of the older generation.

Conclusions

- Recognize the importance of a changing and pluralistic work force and the need for different personnel policies.

- Go for multiskilled, high-performance workers through training, reorganization, and motivation.

- Establish specific programs for upgrading entry-level employees, reducing turnover, hiring experienced seniors, and providing a human, psychologically satisfying work environment.

- Go for high goals of continuous productivity improvement, particularly in the service sector. Shoot for a genuine 10 to 15 percent yearly improvement during the next five years.

- Take a close and unbiased look at the demographics and sensitivity of your top management team and your Board of Directors. Are these people really qualified to understand the new realities of the changing society? Are they genuinely trying to adapt themselves and the business to the new circumstances? Are they just saying the right words, but still clinging to the obsolete status quo?

> *There is nothing more difficult to take in hand, more perilous to conduct, or more uncertain in its success, than to take the lead in the introduction of new things.*
>
> Niccolo Machiavelli (*The Prince*, 1552)

KNOWLEDGE WORKERS

The next structural change is the mix of skilled and unskilled jobs. The demand for knowledge workers will increase (managers, professionals, engineers, technicians, specialists, computer operators). Special skills must be taught. Budgets for training, upgrading, and retraining must increase. The demand for higher wages and better benefits will rise proportionally to the scarcity of skilled personnel. Why should we rely on the more expensive *older* workers? Why not train the new entrants? The majority will be the product of inferior education, often functional illiterates. Many will bear psychological scars of ghetto upbringing, single parents, resentment against society, and poor work habits. Selection and rehabilitation may become too expensive for small and medium businesses to handle.

The above conditions are not assumptions. They are certainties. All the future workers for the next decade are already born. We know their background and education. We also know how many workers will retire or die. We know where the new jobs will be and where they won't. The big question is what to do about it. Executives must decide on the best hiring policies, benefits, motivation, and incentives. They must rethink training and education.

The Knowledge-Dependent Society

A knowledge worker is involved in collecting, analyzing, synthesizing, structuring, storing, retrieving, and using information. Over half of all service workers, 40 million people, and about 80 percent of all managers already belong to this category. As knowledge expands exponentially, the key word becomes *specialization*. Companies will need task-focused specialists in every part of their organization. Our educational system cannot cope with the demand and the diversity. Businesses must train and retrain their own specialists. The halflife of an engineer's knowledge today is five years; soon it will be less than three. Unless technical people are continuously retrained, they'll become obsolete. It's a serious and costly matter. A knowledge worker will soon work 32 hours and learn for 8 hours. Companies must reallocate budgets and resources, devise better, faster training methods, and consider different working and learning environments.

Actions

- Prepare a future skill inventory for your business.

- Devise internal and external training methods to continually upgrade all of your people.

- Initiate better motivation and climate to keep your personnel after a costly investment in their education. There will be openings for 6 million highly skilled occupations. Don't become a free training school for your competitors.

- Put everybody in the company to work to accomplish the transformation. All employees must be involved in the process and must want to participate and contribute.

> *It is better to light one small candle, than to curse the darkness.*
>
> Confucius (400 B.C.)

CORPORATE LOYALTY

Large organizations were proud of their employees' loyalty, dedication, and morale. These were considered the key attributes of corporate success. Times changed. Total employment of Fortune 500 companies is much smaller today than it was 10 years ago. Big companies shed millions of employees. Lifetime employment is gone in America and shrinking in Japan. Employees are aware that job security *ain't what it used to be* and are concerned. Personnel surveys show low employee morale and low job satisfaction. What's the solution?

It's a combination of extremes: *temps* and *core*. Manpower, Inc. is the world's largest temporary employment agency with over 600,000 available workers. They and others dispatch 1.5 million people to do various temporary chores, three times more than a decade ago. But that's just a small part of the 34 million people who work intermittently as self-contractors, supplementals, perdiems, lessees, and peripherals. Part-time workers are not all laborers. They are also doctors, teachers, lawyers, engineers, scientists, accountants, computer specialists, and veterinarians. A small firm specializes in placing temporary CEOs, COOs, and CFOs. Contrary to conventional wisdom, almost 90 percent of part-timers would prefer a steady full-time job. They're the involuntary contingent. Practicality dictates the use of part-time employees to increase organizational flexibility and reduce the break-even point. It's called *accordion management*.

The advantages and disadvantages are many. The company saves on costs of benefits, training, severance pay, and firing hassles. The adverse effects are also obvious. The company faces lack of loyalty, continuity, incentive career advancement, and teamwork. The solution is to compensate for the disadvantages with *core* employees. They're your pool of talent for the *core competencies* absolutely essential in any business. These people must be talented, dedicated, knowledgeable and loyal. They are the people you must love, protect, train, overpay, and coddle. They are the business. They must be treated as individuals in a tailor-made manner. Today's enterprises must operate on both extremes of company loyalty: none and high. The middle is unproductive and dangerous. It's a different world and a different situation. Personnel executives must understand it, adapt to it, and act on it. Do not underestimate the role and the importance of personnel management or compare it to the past. It's a totally new ball game.

> *Business is like an automobile. It won't run itself, except downhill.*
>
> Anon.

COSTLY PERSONNEL TURNOVER

A large, successful, multinational, nonmanufacturing company had a staff turnover of 22 percent! Over 2,000 people worldwide, mostly in sales and distribution, were replaced at an estimated cost of $90 million. That's $45,000 per lost employee! If the company could reduce its personnel turnover, corporate profits would increase by 50 percent each year! Despite continuous attention to the problem, from the CEO down to local countries' managers, little progress has been achieved in the past five years. How can that be?

The problem is not that uncommon. Many multi-outlet service establishments have extremely high turnovers. It's accepted as *normal*, even if it's costly, disruptive, and unproductive. It materially affects sales and customers. Many fast-food services have an annual turnover of 270 percent, hotels 100 percent, banking 50 percent. The cost to employers to replace a worker averages $3,000 for an entry-level employee and $15,000 and more for a professional. A typical hotel with 200 employees spends $600,000 annually on its 100 percent turnover. A Chicago hotel, however, has achieved a relatively low 38 percent annual turnover among its 1,500 full-time employees. Management has instituted a wellness program, training in interpersonal relations, staff meetings, and discussions with employees at all levels. The low turnover shows that providing a caring, quality work environment pays. Yet, few companies do it despite clear expectations of skilled worker shortages.

There are three parts to the solution.

1. *Pre-hiring investment.* Companies are usually eager to fill vacant positions and don't spend enough time and resources to screen applicants. Check your own procedures.

   ➤ Do you give all applicants an extensive questionnaire that may take over two hours to fill out?

   ➤ Do you subject them to an eight-hour battery of psychological and aptitude tests?

   ➤ Do you interview each job seeker at least

twice for a minimum of two hours each time, using several members of your staff?

➤ Do you have a formal evaluation and analysis of results of the 14 to 20 hours spent with each applicant? Companies that apply all this attention (e.g., Toyota in the United States and Britain) have very low turnover rates and very productive employees.

2. *Training.* The era of knowledge requires continuous training and retraining of your personnel. A new employee should receive extensive in-house training for the job he or she will be doing.

➤ Do you have a personalized training program (one to four weeks depending on circumstances and requirements) for each new hire?

➤ Do you have at least two people to check and comment on the progress of the new employee?

➤ Do you carefully follow the progress of each hire for at least a year on the job?

3. *Internal culture and job conditions.* No amount of testing, screening, or training matters, if the new employee becomes unhappy and dissatisfied with the work and the working environment. This is true with multinationals that operate in various countries with different cultures, habits, needs, and wants. It's also true in the United States, where work satisfaction has different parameters in San Francisco, Boise, and Miami. The key to local morale is to understand local differences. One must customize, not standardize, personnel policies and practices. The age of pluralism and indi-

viduality precludes, by definition, a unified, worldwide or even countrywide, policy for wages, rewards, working hours, benefits, rules, and office *ambiance.*

➤ Do you practice decentralized personnel policies, with an understanding of the local conditions and cultural requirements of your employees, including gender, ethnicity, age, marital status, special needs, and competitive pay?

The dogmas of the quiet past are inadequate to the stormy present.

Abraham Lincoln

JOB SATISFACTION

There's a lot of confusion about American workers' morale, attitudes, and performance. Conventional wisdom depicts deep deterioration of satisfaction during the last five years. This is partly true and partly false. Averages don't work in a pluralistic, multifaceted, individualistic society. There are happy and unhappy workers, there are good and bad companies, there are great and lousy jobs. The key is to *customize, not standardize.*

Flexible Policies

Successful management of people in the '90s and beyond will depend on the degree of flexibility of personnel policies and the amount of individual attention accorded to each employee. *Flexible benefits* offer a broad menu of different choices and programs to each worker for personal selection. Already 1200 big companies offer *cafeteria benefits* to their workers. Individual attention to employee needs doesn't have to become a bureaucratic nightmare. Computerized databases can handle individual needs and differences within an equitable cost parameter. Company policies must recognize different needs and wants of a technical person, hourly worker, white-collar clerk, middle manager, or salesperson. We can best encourage teamwork and communications by recognizing personal differences, not by emphasizing uniformity. A step in the right direction is the question: *What do you want?* instead of the statement: *This is what you'll get!*

Challenge and Reward in Flat Organizations

Flat organization and shorter chains of command are essential to faster communications and faster decision making. During the last ten years, U.S. companies eliminated one of every four *middle-management* positions. Layers of management were compressed from 10 or 15 into 4 (e.g., GE). This is a good and necessary trend, but it creates a personnel problem. Fast track (promotion every 18 to 24 months) and upward mobility have slowed to a crawl. Fear of layoffs, reorganizations and restructuring create fear, stifle innovation, and promote buckpassing and action-crippling caution. Many companies have devised innovative policies to help managers adjust to the new realities in the slow lane.

- Reduce the categories of pay scales tied to titles and job descriptions. Widen the pay range for key jobs so individuals can be rewarded without having to be promoted. One large company reduced a 29-tier pay scale to 5, with a broad salary range at each level (e.g., from $33,000 to $74,000).

- Encourage lateral movement and exchanges of managers. It will broaden employees' horizons and knowledge, introduce new challenges and interest. It must be very clear to employees that lateral moves are positive, not dead-end. The express elevator up may be replaced by a zigzagging staircase.

- Increase the responsibility of managers at all levels. Give them more autonomy for decision making. Promote real entrepreneurship at all levels in the organization.

- Tie rewards to performance. Establish meaningful bonuses for exceeding norms in sales, productivity, quality, service, time compression, paperwork reduction, and systems.

- Create dual-track career paths for technicians, engineers, and professionals with pay and benefit incentives for performance, without the need for managerial titles.

Upward mobility has been stymied for the elite group and relatively low numbers of managers. It's also happening to millions of workers who have few chances for promotion and better pay because they lack proper education and training. High-tech society makes continuous education and acquisition of knowledge an absolute must for holding a job with a future. Higher education has raised the pay differential from 15 percent in the '70s to 50 percent today. Low-skill jobs presently pay 18 percent less in real purchasing power than in the early '70s. We must encourage hourly workers to go back to school! They must improve their literacy, their technical skills, and their understanding of computers. Above all, they'll need credible counseling that their future is in their own hands. Union contracts, work rules, and job protection programs will not prevent an accelerated erosion of pay for unskilled and uneducated people.

> *Good people are not expensive, they're priceless.*
>
> Anon.

TEAMWORK

EI stands for employee involvement. It did not originate in Japan. It was used in Sweden, Britain, and the United States long before Japanese auto manufacturers made Quality Circles a household word. American unions are divided on EI. Many vociferously oppose it, while a tepid majority accepts it. But the teamwork concept will grow and expand in scope and acceptance with or without unions' approval. It improves quality and productivity; it reduces costs and supervisory layers; and it foments innovation and self-initiative.

What Is Employee Involvement?

EI no longer represents off-line, problem-solving teams, well known as QC or Quality Circles (group of workers meeting weekly to discuss improvement in quality, productivity, and work conditions). It is not an *ad hoc* task-force team of workers, union representatives, and managers who propose better operations, work reforms, and adaptation to new technology. EI consists of *self-managing teams* in which 5 to 15 employees produce an entire product. They learn all the tasks and skills, rotate responsibilities, plan work schedules, order materials, and manage themselves. Sometimes they decide on their vacation schedules or new hires. Ideally, they run their own small business unit.

The Management Master Series

The Management Master Series offers business managers leading-edge information on the best contemporary management practices. Written by highly respected authorities, each short "briefcase book" addresses a specific topic in a concise, to-the-point presentation, using both text and illustrations. These are ideal books for busy managers who want to get the whole message quickly.

Set 1 — Great Management Ideas

Set 2 — Total Quality

7. *The 16-Point Strategy for Productivity and Total Quality*
William F. Christopher and Carl G. Thor

   Essential points you need to know to improve the performance of your organization.

8. *The TQM Paradigm: Key Ideas That Make It Work*
Derm Barrett

   Get a firm grasp of the world-changing ideas behind the Total Quality movement.

9. *Process Management: A Systems Approach to Total Quality*
Eugene H. Melan

   Learn how a business process orientation will clarify and streamline your organization's capabilities.

10. *Practical Benchmarking for Mutual Improvement*
Carl G. Thor

    Discover a down-to-earth approach to benchmarking and building useful partnerships for quality.

11. *Mistake-Proofing: Designing Errors Out*
Richard B. Chase and Douglas M. Stewart

    Learn how to eliminate errors and defects at the source with inexpensive poka-yoke devices and staff creativity.

12. *Communicating, Training, and Developing for Quality Performance*
Saul W. Gellerman

    Gain quick expertise in communication and employee development basics.

These books are sold in sets. Each set is $85.00 plus $5.00 shipping and handling. Future sets will cover such topics as Customer Service, Leadership, and Innovation. For complete details, call 800-394-6868 or fax 800-394-6286.

BOOKS FROM PRODUCTIVITY PRESS

Productivity Press provides individuals and companies with materials they need to achieve excellence in quality, productivity and the creative involvement of all employees. Through sets of learning tools and techniques, Productivity supports continuous improvement as a vision, and as a strategy. Many of our leading-edge products are direct source materials translated into English for the first time from industrial leaders around the world. Call toll-free 1-800-394-6868 for our free catalog.

Handbook for Productivity Measurement and Improvement
William F. Christopher and Carl G. Thor, eds.
An unparalleled resource! In over 100 chapters, nearly 80 front-runners in the quality movement reveal the evolving theory and specific practices of world-class organizations. Spanning a wide variety of industries and business sectors, they discuss quality and productivity in manufacturing, service industries, profit centers, administration, nonprofit and government institutions, health care and education. Contributors include Robert C. Camp, Peter F. Drucker, Jay W. Forrester, Joseph M. Juran, Robert S. Kaplan, John W. Kendrick, Yasuhiro Monden, and Lester C. Thurow. Comprehensive in scope and organized for easy reference, this compendium belongs in every company and academic institution concerned with business and industrial viability.
ISBN 1-56327-007-2 / 1344 pages / $90.00 / Order HPM-B233

A New American TQM
Four Practical Revolutions in Management
Shoji Shiba, Alan Graham, and David Walden
For TQM to succeed in America, you need to create an American-style "learning organization" with the full commitment and understanding of senior managers and executives. Written expressly for this audience, A *New American TQM* offers a comprehensive and detailed explanation of TQM and how to implement it, based on courses taught at MIT's Sloan School of Management and the Center for Quality Management, a consortium of American companies. Full of case studies and amply illustrated, the book examines major quality tools and how they are being used by the most progressive American companies today.
ISBN 1-56327-032-3 / 606 pages / $50.00 / Order NATQM-B233

Feedback Toolkit
16 Tools for Better Communication in the Workplace
Rick Maurer
In this follow-up to his successful book *Caught in the Middle*, Rick
Maurer explores the issue of feedback by both employer and employee.
Feedback keeps the lines of communication open and serves as a major
motivational tool, yet many managers do not give feedback to their
employees or give it the wrong way. Maurer offers sixteen specific tools
any manager can follow when giving feedback. Written in a fun, easy-to-
read style, this concise book can be read quickly but should be absorbed
slowly and followed carefully. Managing employees must be done
correctly to bring out people's maximum potential. Everyone wants to
know how they're doing. They prefer to hear only the good, but they
know they must hear the bad. In *Feedback Toolkit*, you'll learn how to
dish out the good and the bad, while getting the results you want.
ISBN 1-56327- / [90 pages] / $12.00 / Order FEED-B233

Caught in the Middle
A Leadership Guide for Partnership in the Workplace
Rick Maurer
Managers today are caught between old skills and new expectations.
You're expected not only to improve quality and services, but also to get
staff more involved. This stimulating book provides the inspiration and
know-how to achieve these goals as it brings to light the rewards of
establishing a real partnership with your staff. Includes self-assessment
questionnaires.
ISBN 1-56327-004-8 / 258 pages / $30.00 / Order CAUGHT-B233

TO ORDER: Write, phone, or fax Productivity Press, Dept. BK, P.O. Box 13390, Portland, OR 97213-0390, phone 1-800-394-6868, fax 1-800-394- 6286. Send check or charge to your credit card (American Express, Visa, MasterCard accepted).

U.S. ORDERS: Add $5 shipping for first book, $2 each additional for UPS surface delivery. Add $5 for each AV program containing 1 or 2 tapes; add $12 for each AV program containing 3 or more tapes. We offer attractive quantity discounts for bulk purchases of individual titles; call for more information.

INTERNATIONAL ORDERS: Write, phone, or fax for quote and indicate shipping method desired. For international callers, telephone number is 503-235-0600 and fax number is 503-235-0909. Prepayment in U.S. dollars must accompany your order (checks must be drawn on U.S. banks). When quote is returned with payment, your order will be shipped promptly by the method requested.

NOTE: Prices are in U.S. dollars and are subject to change without notice.

3

FINAL COMMENTS

The determinant of a business success or failure depends on several factors, in a pyramidal form.

1. The ability of the *big boss*, the CEO, to change his/her thinking, habits, and perception of the future.

2. The willpower of the CEO to acquire additional knowledge to guide the executive team intelligently and effectively.

3. The team's ability to communicate and implement the necessary changes throughout the organization.

4. The application of enough resources—time, money, and effort—to retrain and remotivate the entire company's work force.

5. The determination and perseverance to make the changes a continuous way of life, not a one-shot deal.

All businesses face global competition, new technologies, new societies, and changing markets and customers. Some companies will succeed; some will disappear. Economically, it's a zero-sum game; for every winner there must be a loser. But for millions of people, it's their life, their future, and their children's future.

Executives have a responsibility to provide secure employment and hope for advancement for their people. Without them, owners and shareholders have no revenue, no profits, and no future.

> *Leaders are best*
> *When people barely know they exist . . .*
> *When their work is done*
> *Their aim is fulfilled,*
> *People will all say,*
> *We did all this ourselves.*
>
> Lao Tzu (600 B.C.)

ABOUT THE AUTHOR

Dr. Mike Kami was the chief strategic planner for two small companies that made good: IBM and Xerox during their supergrowth years. He retired young and moved to Florida many years ago. But he just couldn't stand still. He became a one-man mini-conglomerate: a combination consultant, writer, public speaker, publisher, boatsman, and entrepreneur.

Dr. Kami is one of the leading business advisers in the world. He has been featured in many magazines and publications in the United States and abroad. His book, *Trigger Points*, was translated into eight languages. *Kami Strategic Assumptions* are published quarterly, advising top executives from leading U.S. and international businesses on latest trends in management practice.